A LOOK AT THE BILL OF RIGHTS

Freedom of the PRESS

BY MARY GRIFFIN

CRASHCOURSE

Gareth Stevens PUBLISHING

Please visit our website, www.garethstevens.com. For a free color catalog of all our high-quality books, call toll free 1-800-542-2595 or fax 1-877-542-2596.

Library of Congress Cataloging-in-Publication Data
Names: Griffin, Mary, 1978- author.
Title: Freedom of the press / Mary Griffin.
Description: Buffalo, New York : Gareth Stevens Publishing, 2026. | Series: A look at the Bill of Rights | Includes index.
Identifiers: LCCN 2024029724 | ISBN 9781482470321 (library binding) | ISBN 9781482470314 (paperback) | ISBN 9781482470338 (ebook)
Subjects: LCSH: Freedom of the press–United States–Juvenile literature. | United States. Constitution. 1st Amendment–Juvenile literature.
Classification: LCC KF4774 .G75 2026 | DDC 323.44/50973–dc23/eng/20240722
LC record available at https://lccn.loc.gov/2024029724

First Edition

Published in 2026 by
Gareth Stevens Publishing
2544 Clinton Street
Buffalo, NY 14224

Designer: Andrea Davison-Bartolotta
Editor: Kristen Rajczak Nelson

Photo credits: Cover, p. 1 Sean Pavone/Shutterstock.com; series art (interior background texture) Nik Merkulov/Shutterstock.com; series art (fact box sticker) Sulovsky/Shutterstock.com; series art (blue backgrounds) Le Chernina/Shutterstock.com; series art (banners) saicle/Shutterstock.com; p. 5 courtesy of the National Archive; pp. 7, 26, 27 courtesy of Library of Congress; p. 9 izzet ugutmen/Shutterstock.com; p. 11 (top) LightField Studios/Shutterstock.com; p. 11 (bottom) Alexander Khitrov/Shutterstock.com; p. 13 File:Boston News Letter, first issue, April 17, 1704.jpg/Wikimedia Commons; p. 15 Elliott Cowand Jr/Shutterstock.com; p. 17 lazyllama/Shutterstock.com; p. 19 wellphoto/Shutterstock.com; p. 21 (all) MKPhoto12/Shutterstock.com; p. 23 Antonio Guillem/Shutterstock.com; p. 25 Denis Makarenko/Shutterstock.com; p. 29 Kaspars Grinvalds/Shutterstock.com.

Printed in China

Some of the images in this book illustrate individuals who are models. The depictions do not imply actual situations or events.

CPSIA compliance information: Batch #QS26GS: For further information contact Gareth Stevens at 1-800-542-2595.

Contents

Words in the glossary appear in **bold** type the first time they are used in the text.

A LIST OF RIGHTS

The U.S. Constitution is the highest law in the United States. At first, the Constitution didn't have a list of rights guaranteed, or promised, to U.S. **citizens**. Many leaders thought this was needed. The Bill of Rights is the name for the first 10 **amendments** to the Constitution.

We the People of the United States, in Order to form a more perfect Union, establish Justice, insure domestic Tranquility, provide for the common defence, promote the general Welfare, and secure the Blessings of Liberty to ourselves and our Posterity, do ordain and establish this Constitution for the United States of America.

Article. I.

Section. 1. All legislative Powers herein granted shall be vested in a Congress of the United States, which shall consist of a Senate and House of Representatives.

Make the GRADE

A constitution lists the most basic laws of a country or state. The U.S. Constitution has been in use since 1789.

James Madison put forward a list of amendments that would protect, or keep safe, citizens' rights. Congress sent 12 of these to the states. The states approved, or agreed to, 10 of them. The Bill of Rights became part of the Constitution in 1791.

Make the GRADE

James Madison played a big part in writing the Constitution. He found that the promise of individual rights was needed to get states' approval of it—so he wrote amendments that protected those rights!

James Madison, Congress member from Virginia and fourth U.S. president

THE FIRST AMENDMENT

The First Amendment states in part: "Congress shall make no law . . . abridging the freedom of speech, or of the press." This means the government can't make laws that take away or **weaken** citizens' ability to say or **publish** their ideas, or opinions.

Make the GRADE

The First Amendment also says citizens have the right to practice any religion, or faith, they want and to peacefully assemble, or gather.

WHAT IS THE PRESS?

The Constitution does not say what the "press" is. "Press" is commonly used to mean journalists, or people whose job it is to report the news in newspapers, on TV, or online. Freedom of the press has been used to protect any publisher.

Make the GRADE

The "media" is another word for the press. Media can mean the outlets and people who cover the news.

WHY INCLUDE IT?

Early Americans believed freedom of the press was very important. When the United States was still part of Great Britain, the British government tried to **censor** newspapers. It didn't want colonists publishing **criticism** or views against the British government.

N. E. Numb. 1

The Boſton News-Letter.

Publiſhed by Authority.

From Monday April 17. to Monday April 24. 1704.

London Flying-Poſt from *Decemb. 2d.* to *4th.* 1703.

LEtters from *Scotland* bring us the Copy of a Sheet lately Printed there, Intituled, *A ſeaſonable Alarm for* Scotland. *In a Letter from a Gentleman in the City, to his Friend in the Country, concerning the preſent Danger of the Kingdom and of the Proteſtant Religion.*

This Letter takes Notice, That Papiſts ſwarm in that Nation, that they traffick more avowedly than formerly, and that of late many Scores of Prieſts & Jeſuites are come thither from France, and gone to the North, to the Highlands & other places of the Country. That the Miniſters of the Highlands and North gave in large Liſts of them to the Committee of the General Aſſembly, to be laid before the Privy-Council.

It likewiſe obſerves, that a great Number of other ill-affected perſons are come over from *France*, under pretence of accepting her Majeſty's Gracious Indemnity; but, in reality, to increaſe Diviſions in the Nation, and to entertain a Correſpondence with *France*: That their ill Intentions are evident from their talking big, their owning the Intereſt of the pretended King *James* VIII. their ſecret Cabals, and their buying up of Arms and Ammunition, wherever they can find them.

To this he adds the late Writinge and Actings of ſome diſaffected perſons, many of whom are for that Pretender; that ſeveral of them have declar'd they had rather embrace Popery than conform to the preſent Government; that they refuſe to pray for the Queen, but uſe the ambiguous word Soveraign, and ſome of them pray in expreſs Words for the King and Royal Family; and the charitable and generous Prince who has ſhew'd them ſo much Kindneſs. He likewiſe takes notice of Letters, not long ago found in Cypher, & directed to a Perſon lately come thither from St. *Germains*.

He ſays that the greateſt Jacobites, who will not qualifie themſelves by taking the Oaths to Her Majeſty, do now with the Papiſts and their Companions from St. *Germains* ſet up for the Liberty of the Subject, contrary to their own Principles, but meerly to keep up a Diviſion in the Nation. He adds, that they aggravate thoſe things which the People complain of, as to *England's* refuſing to allow them a freedom of Trade, *&c.* and do all they can to foment Diviſions betwixt the Nations, & to obſtruct a Redreſs of thoſe things complain'd of.

The Jacobites, he ſays, do all they can to perſuade the Nation that their pretended King is a Proteſtant in his Heart, tho' he dares not declare it while under the Power of *France*; that he is acquainted with the Miſtakes of his Father's Government, will govern us more according to Law, and endear himſelf to his Subjects.

They magnifie the Strength of their own Party, and the Weakneſs and Diviſions of the other, in order to facilitate and haſte their Undertaking; they argue themſelves out of their Fears, and into the higheſt aſſurance of accompliſhing their purpoſe.

From all this he infers, That they have hopes of Aſſiſtance from *France*, otherwiſe they would never be ſo impudent; and he gives Reaſons for his Apprehenſions that the *French* King may ſend Troops thither this Winter, 1. Becauſe the *Engliſh* & *Dutch* will not then be at Sea to oppoſe them. 2. He can then beſt ſpare them, the Seaſon of Action beyond Sea being over. 3. The Expectation given him of a conſiderable number to joyn them, may incourage him to the undertaking with fewer Men, if he can but ſend over a ſufficient number of Officers with Arms and Ammunition.

He endeavours in the reſt of his Letters to anſwer the fooliſh Pretences of the Pretender's being a Proteſtant, and that he will govern us according to Law. He ſays, that being bred up in the Religion and Politicks of *France*, he is by Education a ſtated Enemy to our Liberty and Religion. That the Obligations which he and his Family owe to the *French* King, muſt neceſſarily make him to be wholly at his Devotion, and to follow his Example; that if he ſit upon the Throne, the three Nations muſt be oblig'd to pay the Debt which he owes the *French* King for the Education of himſelf, and for Entertaining his ſuppoſed Father and his Family. And ſince the King muſt reſtore him by his Troops, if ever he be reſtored, he will ſee to ſecure his own Debt, before thoſe Troops leave *Britain*. The Pretender being a good Proficient in the *French* and *Romiſh* Schools, he will never think himſelf ſufficiently aveng'd, but by the utter Ruine of his Proteſtant Subjects, both as Hereticks and Traitors. The late Queen, his pretended Mother, who in cold Blood when ſhe was Queen of *Britain*, advis'd to turn the Weſt of *Scotland* into a hunting Field; will be then for doing ſo by the greateſt part of the Nation; and, no doubt, is at Pains to have her pretended Son educated to her own Mind: Therefore, he ſays, it were a great Madneſs in the Nation to take a Prince bred up in the horrid School of Ingratitude, Perſecution and Cruelty, and filled with Rage and Envy. The *Jacobites*, he ſays, both in *Scotland* and at St. *Germains*, are impatient under their preſent Straits, and knowing their Circumſtances cannot be much worſe than they are, at preſent, are the more inclinable to the Undertaking. He adds, That the *French* King knows there cannot be a more effectual way for himſelf to arrive at the Univerſal Monarchy, and to ruine the Proteſtant Intereſt, than by ſetting up the Pretender upon the Throne of Great *Britain*, he will in all probability attempt it; and tho' he ſhould be perſuaded that the Deſign would miſcarry in the cloſe, yet he cannot but reap ſome Advantage by imbroiling the three Nations.

From all this the Author concludes it to be the Intereſt of the Nation, to provide for Self defence; and ſays, that as many have already taken the Alarm, and are furniſhing themſelves with Arms and Ammunition, he hopes the Government will not only allow it, but encourage it, ſince the Nation ought all to appear as one Man in the Defen

Make the GRADE

In 1776, Virginia became the first state to protect freedom of the press in the Virginia Declaration of Rights.

STILL IMPORTANT TODAY

The press gives the public facts it needs to know. It reports wrongdoing—even that of the government. It allows for all sides of an **issue** to be heard. The First Amendment protects the press from being **punished** for what it publishes.

Make the GRADE

The press is sometimes called the "watchdog" of the government. It not only reports news about the government, but also gives criticism of it.

BRINGING IN THE COURT

The Supreme Court is the highest court in the United States. It **interprets** the Constitution as it hears cases about the First Amendment. It decides whether laws or actions are constitutional, or follow the Constitution. It may decide something is unconstitutional too.

Make the GRADE

Freedom of the press is closely tied to freedom of speech. Many Supreme Court cases about freedom of speech have had to do with freedom of the press.

The Supreme Court and lower courts have decided many cases that have made the meaning of "freedom of the press" clearer. In general, if what the press reported is true and the facts were gathered lawfully, the press is protected.

Make the GRADE

Libel is the publishing of untrue facts about a person that cause them harm. Libel is not protected by the First Amendment.

CENSORSHIP

The First Amendment protects the press against government censorship. Censorship is the removal of published items believed to be harmful. Book bans are a form of censorship. But, the only Supreme Court ruling about them wasn't broad enough to stop them everywhere.

Make the GRADE

Ideas and opinions that seem unkind are protected under the First Amendment. The government cannot stop them from being published.

art spiegelman
MAUS
BANNED
THE #1 NEW YORK TIMES BESTSELLER
JASON REYNOLDS
IBRAM X. KENDI
BANNED
BANNED
PENGUIN CLASSICS
JOHN STEINBECK
Of Mice and Men

FREE PRESS LIMITS

Freedom of the press has some **limits**, such as within schools. In *Hazelwood v. Kuhlmeier*, the Supreme Court sided with a principal who censored articles to be published in the school paper. It decided the principal had not **violated** students' First Amendment rights.

Make the GRADE

The Supreme Court said student newspapers could be censored if articles were seen as **inappropriate** or could stop the school from running smoothly.

Concern, or worry, about national security may limit freedom of the press. The government may believe the publication of certain facts could put the country in danger. However, this reasoning does not often stop the press from publishing.

Make the GRADE

The freedoms in the Bill of Rights have always been guaranteed by the national government. When the 14th Amendment passed, state governments also had to guarantee these rights.

Canon

THE PENTAGON PAPERS

In 1971, the U.S. government tried to stop the *New York Times* and the *Washington Post* from publishing documents, or papers, they had been given by a government worker. The papers were **classified**. The Supreme Court said this was a violation of freedom of the press!

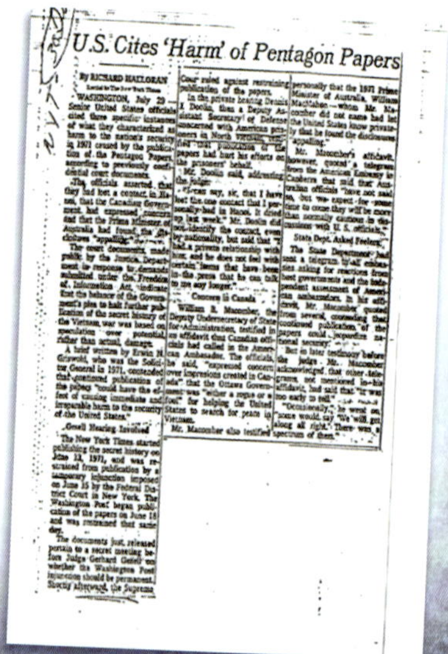
U.S. Cites 'Harm' of Pentagon Papers

New York Times article about the Pentagon Papers

Make the GRADE

The documents became known as the "Pentagon Papers." The Pentagon is the main building for the U.S. Department of Defense, which oversees national security.

announcement of outcome of Pentagon Papers court case, June 30, 1971

PRESS IN THE FUTURE

Today, the idea of the press is changing. Most people get news online—and not always from a trained journalist. Still, the protections of the First Amendment do not end online. The Supreme Court continues to interpret freedom of the press for the future!

Make the GRADE

Social media are websites and applications, also known as apps, used to create online communities. The press may post on social media as part of their job, but anyone can make a post with their opinion.

THINK ABOUT IT!

Read the following stories and think about what you've read. How would you apply citizens' First Amendment rights to freedom of the press?

A student writes an article for the school newspaper's website. They post it before the journalism teacher can read it. The teacher takes the article down and asks the student to make changes. *Were the student's First Amendment rights violated?*

A newspaper reporter has a file showing the mayor has stolen money from the city. The file was from the mayor's personal computer—but the reporter didn't take the file. The file was given to them by a person who worked for the mayor. The newspaper publishes an article about the stolen money. *Is the newspaper protected by freedom of the press?*

Jessica posts a video on Tik Tok about everything she dislikes about the U.S. president. *Is she now part of the press? Why or why not?*

Glossary

amendment: A change or addition to a constitution.

censor: To look at newspapers, books, movies, letters, or other published pieces to remove what is thought to be inappropriate or harmful.

citizen: Someone who lives in a country legally and has certain rights.

classified: Being secret to all but a few people in a government.

criticism: Showing disapproval of and pointing out the problems of a person or thing.

inappropriate: Not well suited to a time, place, or audience.

interpret: To tell the meaning of something.

issue: An important topic that people care about.

limit: To stop something from being larger, longer, or more.

publish: To make a book, magazine, or other written content for people to read.

punish: To make someone suffer for wrongdoing, such as through jail time or a fine.

violate: To do something that is not allowed by law.

weaken: To make less strong.

For More Information

Books

Matulli, Allison, and Clelia Castro-Malaspina. *Your Freedom, Your Power: A Kid's Guide to the First Amendment*. Philadelphia, PA: Running Press Kids, 2023.

Keppeler, Jill. *What Is the First Amendment?* Buffalo, NY: Rosen Publishing, 2023.

Website

Bill of Rights
https://bensguide.gpo.gov/bill-of-rights-1789-91
Check out this short guide to all the amendments included in the Bill of Rights.

Publisher's note to educators and parents: Our editors have carefully reviewed these websites to ensure that they are suitable for students. Many websites change frequently, however, and we cannot guarantee that a site's future contents will continue to meet our high standards of quality and educational value. Be advised that students should be closely supervised whenever they access the internet.

Index